CHARITIES IN ACTION

SAVING THE ENVIRONMENT

Andrew Langley

Heinemann
LIBRARY

Chicago, Illinois

www.capstonepub.com
Visit our website to find out more information about Heinemann-Raintree books.

To order:
☏ Phone 800-747-4992
🖥 Visit www.capstonepub.com to browse our catalog and order online.

Edited by Andrew Farrow, Adam Miller, and Diyan Leake
Designed by Victoria Allen
Picture research by Ruth Blair
Illustrations by Oxford Designers & Illustrators
Production by Victoria Fitzgerald

Originated by Capstone Global Library Ltd
Printed and bound in China by Leo Paper Products Ltd

16 15 14 13 12
10 9 8 7 6 5 4 3 2 1

Library of Congress Cataloging-in-Publication Data
Langley, Andrew, 1949-
  Saving the environment / Andrew Langley.—1st ed.
    p. cm.—(Charities in action)
  Includes bibliographical references and index.
  ISBN 978-1-4329-6389-7 (hb)—ISBN 978-1-4329-6396-5 (pb) 1. Voluntarism. 2. Environmentalism. 3. Charity organization. 4. Social participation. I. Title.
  HN49.V64.L37 2013
    361.3'7—dc23   2012000691

Acknowledgments
The author and publisher are grateful to the following for permission to reproduce copyright material: Alamy pp. 17 (© Tryphosa Ho), 29 (© Mark Conlin), 33 (© Penny Tweedie), 34 (© Keith Morris), 39 (© Lana Rastro), 41 (© AF archive); Bush Heritage Australia p. 49 (© Peter Morris); Corbis pp. 9 (© Robert Van Der Berge/Sygma), 11 (© Phil Klein), 13 (© Narendra Shrestha/epa), 21 (© Greenpeace/epa), 25 (© Ralph Clevenger), 31 (© Andrew Lichtenstein), 45 (© Noel Hendrickson/Blend Images), 51 (© David Brabyn), 52 (© Jiang Fan/Xinhua Press), 55 (© Tim Pannell), 57 (© Alain Felix/Hemis); Earthwatch p. 47 (Simon Wallace); © Friends of the Earth International p. 5; courtesy of Fundación ProAves (www.proaves.org) p. 19; Getty Images pp. 27 (Sion Touhig), 37 (Robert Harding World Imagery/Michael Runkel); © Dave Lauridsen p. 22; The Wilderness Society p. 43.

Cover photograph of divers collecting octocorals for the Queensland Museum collection as part of the Coral Life census, Lizard Island, Queensland, Australia, April 2008, reproduced with permission of Naturepl (© Jurgen Freund).

Every effort has been made to contact copyright holders of material reproduced in this book. Any omissions will be rectified in subsequent printings if notice is given to the publisher.

Disclaimer
All the Internet addresses (URLs) given in this book were valid at the time of going to press. However, due to the dynamic nature of the Internet, some addresses may have changed, or sites may have changed or ceased to exist since publication. While the author and publisher regret any inconvenience this may cause readers, no responsibility for any such changes can be accepted by either the author or the publisher.

CONTENTS

World in Danger 4

Planning for Action 10

Going Global 16

Community Conservation 24

Educating for Change 32

Money and Publicity 38

Research 44

A Vision for the Future 50

Volunteering 54

Facts and Figures 58

Glossary 60

Find Out More 62

Index 64

Words printed in **bold** are explained in the glossary.

WORLD IN DANGER

Our environment is under threat. **Ice caps** are melting, seas are rising, and the climate is changing. Drought, earthquakes, and storms are becoming more frequent. Fuel is running out, and water and air are being polluted. Many animal and plant species are disappearing. Can we do anything to stop this process? Thousands of people who work for environmental charities all over the world believe we can.

People and pollution: Caroline's story

Caroline Ntaopane is a volunteer. She works for a charity near Johannesburg, in South Africa. Its aim is to make sure that people in the local community are treated fairly when major industries cause **pollution** in their environment.

Caroline has to face environmental problems every day. She lives just 328 feet (100 meters) from a giant chemical plant in the Vaal region. She sees the smoke filling the sky and the roar of the flares burning waste gas. She feels the machines shaking the ground under her feet, and she smells the stench of the chemicals. Many neighbors, including members of her own family, have breathing problems due to the pollution.

In 2005, Caroline helped launch the Vaal Environment Justice Alliance (VEJA). This represents local environmental groups, which work together to tackle the damage caused by chemical and steel companies in the area. For many years, waste from their plants has been polluting air and water sources, and the government has done little to regulate them.

The VEJA measures air and water quality in the area, **monitors** how waste is managed, and checks the health of local people and company workers. Caroline oversees the monitoring, organizes meetings, and publicizes the work of the charity. There is not enough money to pay someone to run the office, so she does most of the paperwork as well.

Working for change

What inspired Caroline to volunteer for an environmental charity? The turning point came in 2002, when she visited the United States. Here she saw how pollution affects everyone—but those who suffer the most harm are usually poor, black, and disadvantaged. This is also especially true in parts of South Africa, where many black people live in poverty. "I really want to see change happen," she says, "and I have the experience, passion, and capabilities to help bring about that change." Sometimes it feels as if she is struggling against huge obstacles and getting nowhere. "But I know we are making a difference," she says.

There are many thousands of people like Caroline Ntaopane all over the world, who have dedicated themselves to doing something positive about the massive problems facing our environment. Some have full-time jobs with environmental charities or other **nonprofit organizations**. Others work for free in their spare time. You will meet many of them throughout this book.

Caroline Ntaopane campaigns for better air quality for all in the Vaal region of South Africa.

What are the major threats to the environment?

The world's **ecosystems** are being damaged in many ways. Most of these ways are connected. Scientists agree that human activity is the main cause of the damage. Here are some of the biggest threats:

- *Climate change*: Earth's atmosphere is getting warmer, due partly to a buildup of **carbon** gases. This causes ice caps to melt, leading to a rise in sea levels.

- *The energy crisis*: **Fossil fuels** (such as coal and petroleum) will soon run out. New and **sustainable** ways of generating energy will have to be developed.

- *Pollution*: Modern society produces chemicals and waste that poison soil, air, and water. Industry and agriculture are among the biggest polluters.

- *Population growth*: The world's population is growing faster every year. We need to produce more food and other essentials and also cope with more waste.

- *Disappearing farmland*: Climate change, pollution, and other factors are ruining large areas of land. These can no longer be used for growing food.

Governments and greenness

Who can solve these problems, which endanger the future of life on this planet? One answer is international agencies such as the United Nations (UN), which can reach all corners of the world. This organization runs a massive project called the United Nations Environment Program (UNEP), which helps **developing countries** to protect their environments.

Many national governments work to combat threats to the environment. But they find it difficult to agree with other governments about how to deal with the threats. They are also under pressure from industrial and business leaders not to take actions that might harm the **economy**.

Most **developed countries** have their own agencies devoted to "green" and conservation issues. In the United States, there is the Environmental Protection Agency (EPA), which enforces rules on matters such as air and water quality.

Getting warmer

In its 2007 report, the global agency Intergovernmental Panel on Climate Change (IPCC) showed how dramatically Earth's atmosphere is heating up. For example:

• The period 1995 to 2006 contained 11 of the hottest 12 years since records began.

• Between 1993 and 2003, sea levels rose by an average of 0.12 inch (3.1 millimeters) a year.

• The area of ice in the Arctic is shrinking by an average of 2.7 percent each decade.

Different environments all over the world are under threat. This map shows some of the areas studied in this book, as well as places where research is going on to find solutions.

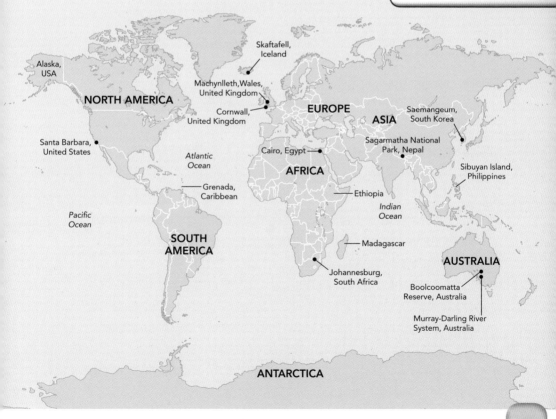

Charities make a difference

Charities have a very special role to play in dealing with environmental problems. There are several hundred charities throughout the world devoted to tackling a wide range of environmental issues. Every one is created and run by people who are genuinely committed to making the world a "greener" place. They are funded by donations from individuals, corporations, and governments.

What makes charities different? For a start, they are usually private and independent (unlike most politicians) and so are not influenced by governments or big businesses. They are also not-for-profit organizations, which means that they do not have to give surplus wealth to shareholders. Instead, they use it to carry out their programs.

Global and local

Some of the larger environmental charities, such as Friends of the Earth or ActionAid, are global bodies. They operate in many parts of the world and are involved in many different types of activity. Charities like this are well known through advertising and news stories, and they draw enormous sums in donations each year.

Many other charities are less famous and work on a smaller scale. Some, such as the Chesapeake Bay Foundation in the eastern United States, are concerned with the conservation of a specific area. Others are focused on a single kind of activity, such as promoting **solar energy**, planting trees, or protecting a specific animal species or **habitat**.

What do charities do?

Environmental charities do not all work in the same way. There is a huge variety of methods for achieving their specific aims. Among these are:

• *Practical help*: Some charities give assistance to those people who are worst affected by pollution, energy shortages, or many other problems caused by climate change.

• *Education*: Some charities inform and alert the public about threats to the environment, their impact on our lives, and how they can be dealt with.

• *Conservation*: Some charities restore and protect habitats that have suffered damage.

• *Direct action*: Some charities challenge and obstruct projects that may pose serious dangers to people and ecosystems.

Greenpeace activists chained themselves to railroad tracks to disrupt the transportation of nuclear waste. The yellow box is difficult to remove and delayed the train.

Different ways to help the planet: Dateline, June 2011

1. "GLOBAL CHARITY'S GOAL TO PLANT ONE MILLION TREES"

With this headline, the Plant a Tree Today Foundation (PATT) launched an ambitious plan. The charity aims to plant one million new trees in Thailand, Indonesia, and other Asian countries. These will restore forests that have been cut down, not only helping local people but also fighting against climate change caused by the loss of native habitats.

At one end of the process is Runrueng Lengwilas, who runs the plant nursery in Sap Tai, Thailand, where thousands of new trees are grown. He is also an experienced nature guide. At the other end are the bands of PATT employees and volunteers who clear scrub and actually plant the trees.

2. "GREENPEACE BLOCK NUCLEAR WASTE SHIPMENT"

Activists from the charity Greenpeace International made a dramatic protest against **nuclear energy** in the Netherlands. Ten Greenpeace volunteers chained themselves to the railroad track in order to stop a train carrying **radioactive** waste materials to be processed in France.

Which kind of action against environmental threats do you think is more effective? How dramatic do antinuclear protests have to be to get noticed?

9

PLANNING FOR ACTION

Starting an environmental charity is a huge challenge. Keeping it going, and making it successful and effective over a long period, is even tougher. The challenge is even bigger at times of global economic hardship, when people and governments have less money to donate to good causes.

Setting up

What are the most important things needed to plan and launch a new charity?

• *A clear vision:* The founders have to know exactly what their values and aims are and have a realistic plan of action for achieving them.

• *Lots of research*: Are there charities out there already doing the same sort of work for the environment? It does not make sense to simply duplicate campaigns. It could damage established organizations as well as the new one.

• *The right staff:* Volunteers and other workers have to be dedicated to the goals of the charity, be prepared to work hard, and feel enthusiastic about what they do.

• *Funds up front:* It should be able to pay workers and set up programs as soon as possible. This means surviving without donations at first, because many people are unwilling to give money to an organization with no track record.

• *Getting the paperwork done:* Most countries have strict rules about how charities should be founded and run. They have to have a written set of rules and a board of trustees, which is a group of people who oversee the charity's work.

Moving forward

Steering a charity through good and bad years demands enthusiasm and passion. But, like any other business, it must also be run professionally. Managers have to be familiar with regulations concerning nonprofit organizations. They should make regular reviews of progress, to make sure they are sticking to their original vision.

Charities aim to explain clearly what they are doing. So they publish regular reports about their activities, research findings, education programs, and publicity campaigns. They also have daily office work to do, including recruiting and training staff, ordering materials, and keeping in contact with people working in the field.

Making a living

Charities deal with other people's money, so they have to manage their finances carefully. Donations should be used in the most efficient way. How much should be spent on fieldwork, and how much on advertising? How much should workers be paid? Charity workers generally earn less than most people, but they still need enough to live on.

On top of this, the charity has to live within its means. Setting a realistic **budget** for spending each year, and sticking to it, is very important. Detailed accounts must also be kept of money coming in and going out.

How many charities?

The number of charities throughout the world is mind-boggling. There are at least 1.1 million in the United States alone, of which over 300 are involved in issues connected to helping the environment.

Demonstrators carry signs protesting against the Diablo Canyon Power Plant during the Mothers for Peace Nuke Protest in Avila Beach, California, in April 2011.

Friends of the Earth International

Friends of the Earth International (FoEI) is the biggest environmental network of them all. It campaigns for a huge variety of urgent environmental and social issues all over the world. It is also one of the oldest environmental organizations; its 40th anniversary was in 2011.

How is the network organized?

FoEI is not just one charity, but rather a vast group of them, covering every continent and 76 countries. Its members include over 5,000 local activist groups, and it has more than 2 million members and supporters. The network is supported by its headquarter's office in Amsterdam, in the Netherlands.

The main targets for FoEI

• *Agrofuels*: Energy companies are grabbing land in developing countries to grow fuel crops instead of food. FoEI educates people about the dangers of this and urges financial institutions to stop supporting the agrofuels sector.

• *Climate justice and energy*: The world faces **global warming** and an energy crisis due to wasteful fuel use by some countries. FoEI works for the right of all people to have an equal share in energy resources.

• *Food sovereignty*: FoEI believes people should be able to control their own food systems. It supports small peasant farmers against the power of big corporations, which often destroy their livelihoods.

• *Forests and biodiversity*: The world's forests are being destroyed to provide timber, farmland, and other products. Member groups work with local communities to manage forest resources and campaign against the exploitation of forests.

• *Resisting mining*: The search for fossil fuels causes many environmental disasters. FoEI groups support communities damaged by this and challenge governments to find alternative and sustainable energy sources.

FoEI in action

FoEI members take part in many hundreds of environmental campaigns all over the world. A few examples are listed on the opposite page.

Australia

The Murray–Darling River system in Victoria is drying up, as a result of climate change and water extraction. Activist groups are campaigning to save it. They want the government to buy back water licenses from farmers and other water users.

Nepal

Melting glaciers threaten the famous Everest (Sagarmatha) National Park. FoE Nepal has helped draw up a petition to protect the area. It was supported by climber Sir Edmund Hillary (one of the first people to climb Everest, the world's highest peak) and conservationist David Attenborough.

South Korea

FoE Korea and other groups are pressuring the government to halt a land reclamation plan on the Saemangeum tidal flats. This is destroying a beautiful part of Korea's coastline and an important **wetland** ecosystem.

Uganda

A Ugandan environmental organization is working to stop mining companies from illegally quarrying limestone and drilling for oil in protected areas such as national parks and the Rift Valley.

One of the greatest environmental threats to Nepal is caused by global warming. This has melted snow high in the Himalayas, which swells mountain lakes and increases the threat of serious flooding.

Green workers

Big or small, local or global, a charity needs skilled workers to run it. At the top are the directors or trustees. These people are independent and unpaid and are usually experts in the kind of work the charity does. They make the big decisions about the group's campaigns and finances. These decisions are put into effect by the chief executive officer, who is in charge of the daily coordinating of the organization.

The rest of the workforce is usually divided into two parts. One includes all the people who work in the field, either overseas or locally. They may do a huge variety of tasks, from running projects to collecting information.

The second part includes the administrative staff. They support the field workers, raise funds, control the finances, and run the charity's offices.

What skills are needed?

People want to work for an environmental charity because they are committed to its causes. But good charity workers need more than passion and enthusiasm. They will also have to work with others and make their own decisions. So they should be reliable, sensible, and self-confident. They should also be self-motivated and good at communicating and organizing.

Being an intern

Some environmental charities take on young people for periods of work experience, which are usually unpaid. These are called internships. An **intern** is generally a college student or college graduate, or in some cases a high-school student, with a real interest in environmental matters.

An internship can last from a few months to a year or more. In that time, the intern may take part in a job that will help him or her develop personal skills and learn about how a charity works. Areas of work for interns include event planning, public relations, regional conservation, **archives**, and more.

Conserving traditional communities

In 2011, Jennifer Hanlon was an intern for the Alaska Conservation Foundation. Her internship lasted for 12 weeks of the summer, during which she gathered information about the culture of the area. Jennifer was born and raised in Alaska. She grew up in a traditional hunting community where people still live off the land, so she is interested in the way our natural environment defines how we live. She believes that ecosystems have to be healthy to support people who live in close harmony with the land.

How a big global charity works

A big charity, such as Conservation International, works on a large number of projects worldwide. To do this effectively, it needs a large workforce (400 at headquarters and nearly 600 in the field). It also needs a strong structure. This diagram shows the staffing structure of Conservation International:

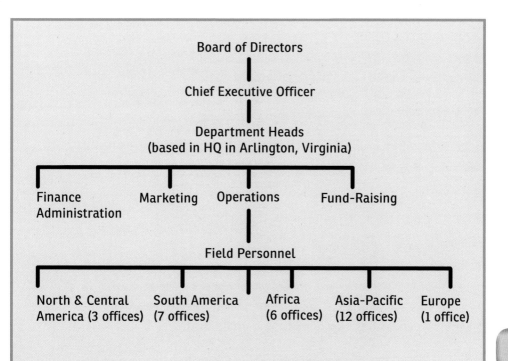

Board of Directors

Chief Executive Officer

Department Heads
(based in HQ in Arlington, Virginia)

Finance Administration   Marketing   Operations   Fund-Raising

Field Personnel

North & Central America (3 offices)   South America (7 offices)   Africa (6 offices)   Asia-Pacific (12 offices)   Europe (1 office)

GOING GLOBAL

The best-known environmental charities are usually the biggest ones, such as Greenpeace, ActionAid, or WWF. Their publicity campaigns and appeals are seen all over the world and raise huge amounts of money each year. This is spent on big projects in most parts of the developing world. They employ hundreds of people and have offices in major cities.

Across the planet

The large charities have many ways of working—giving practical help, giving financial or expert support, campaigning, or just raising public awareness. Here are some examples of big organizations using their money and knowledge to help provide solutions to major environmental problems.

Global warming

What's the problem? The world is getting hotter, due largely to the buildup of carbons in the atmosphere.

Who's tackling it? The Rainforest Alliance works to preserve the huge forest ecosystems in tropical areas, which act as natural storage organs for carbon, thus keeping it out of the atmosphere. The alliance supports farmers and companies who use rain forest products in a sustainable way.

Sustainable farming

What's the problem? Many modern farming practices damage the environment, causing land **degradation** and pollution.

Who's tackling it? The Soil Association has been promoting more environmentally friendly ways of farming. These include the use of organic fertilizers, the reform of intensive systems such as caged poultry, and closer ties between farmers and their communities.

Alternative energy sources

What's the problem? The world needs to find renewable sources of energy to replace fossil and nuclear fuels.

Who's tackling it? The Wilderness Society in the United States has backed a massive solar power project on the Crescent Dunes area of Nevada. This will help the state to generate more electricity, while lowering its **emissions** of carbon (from burning fossil fuels).

Some charities support farmers who grow food using organic methods, such as these vegetable and rice crops in East Java, Indonesia.

Damaged ecosystems

What's the problem? The world's fragile ecosystems are being damaged or destroyed by climate change, natural disasters, and other threats.

Who's tackling it? Wetlands International works to preserve and restore the wetland areas of the world. One of its projects is helping local communities in Aceh, Indonesia, to replant their mangrove forest ecosystem.

Aldo Leopold (1887–1948), pioneering conservationist and ecologist

As a young man, Aldo Leopold worked for the Forest Service in Arizona and New Mexico. One of his duties was to shoot predators such as bears and mountain lions. He soon learned to respect the place of such animals in their environment, and he went on to recommend the preservation of wildlife habitats in the United States. In 1935, he was one of the founders of the Wilderness Society, pledging to protect the country's wilderness areas. His book *A Sand County Almanac* became a best seller after his death. He stated that:

"We abuse land because we regard it as a commodity belonging to us. When we see land as a community to which we belong, we may begin to use it with love and respect."

The World Land Trust: Securing the rain forests

The rain forests of Latin America are disappearing fast. Logging, mining, and agriculture destroy huge areas every year. How can they be saved? The obvious answer is to buy them. This is the aim of the World Land Trust (WLT), based in the United States and the United Kingdom. Since 1989, the charity has raised enough money to purchase over 1.7 million acres (680,000 hectares) of endangered forest—an area bigger than the state of Delaware. This keeps it safe—forever.

David Attenborough, who is a patron of the World Land Trust, says: "You will not save endangered species unless you save the whole ecosystem. And to save an ecosystem you need to save the land. That is what WLT's project partners do."

Buy an acre

The WLT has a simple offer to make. One acre of threatened land costs, on average, about $150. Anyone who donates this sum has saved an acre of rain forest. Smaller donations from individuals, and much larger ones from businesses and other organizations, are also collected to purchase land in vulnerable areas from private owners.

The charity works very efficiently. Of the money it raises, only about 3 percent is spent on administration. This means that over 96 percent goes toward buying and helping to preserve as much rain forest as possible.

Partners in the project

The WLT does not buy large chunks of rain forest directly. It works through local conservation groups, which negotiate the deals with the owners. The charity selects these partners carefully, to make sure they have the right motives, skills, and experience.

The WLT provides the money to pay for the land. But once the land has been secured, it does not belong to the charity. Rather, it is owned by the local partner groups, who manage the site and are responsible for protecting it. The WLT gives them support and expert advice about conservation and research. Such deals depend on one thing: money. Without enough donations, the WLT would not be able to buy anything or train people to protect the sites.

What's been saved?

Since it was founded in 1989, the WLT has raised enough money to preserve important rain forest habitats, including:

- *Peru*: Reserves protect communities of **indigenous** Amazonian peoples.
- *Bolivia*: A giant nature reserve protects some of the world's most endangered species of birds.
- *Ecuador*: Unique "cloud" forests high in the Andes are preserved.
- *Chile*: An ecosystem that contains some of the world's oldest trees has been preserved.
- *Venezuela*: About 40,000 acres (16,000 hectares) of forest and grassland have been preserved.

Paul Salaman of WLT is shown with children in the community of Puerto Pinzón, a village in Boyacá, Colombia.

Dr. Paul Salaman: the trust's director of conservation

At the age of eight, Paul met the famous broadcaster and natural history writer (and later WLT patron) David Attenborough. This meeting inspired him to become a naturalist and conservationist. At age 14, he was already managing a small nature reserve in London, England. As a student, he led expeditions across Colombia, finding several birds new to science. He helped found the El Dorado Nature Reserve there, which he calls "the ultimate Noah's Ark, protecting the last populations of many critically endangered flora and fauna; a living treasure trove like no other on Earth." Paul has worked for the World Land Trust since 2008.

Same goal—different methods

The buying of threatened land is an effective plan for saving threatened rain forest areas. But this is just one method of campaigning to save our environment. There are many global green charities, and they have many different ways of achieving their aims. Some give practical help to prevent damage. Some raise money to repair damage that is already done. Others take direct action to protest against people they see as environmental villains.

Two ways of fighting the fuel crisis

Direct confrontation

On June 17, 2011, activists from Greenpeace International landed on an oil-drilling platform operated by Cairn Energy off the Arctic coast of Greenland. As the activists climbed the 98-foot (30-meter) ladder, rig crew members tried to drive them back with sprays of freezing water. When they reached the platform, the activists were arrested.

Why did Greenpeace do it? Its leader, Kumi Naidoo, said, "Because Arctic oil drilling is one of the defining environmental battles of our age. The rapidly melting cap of Arctic sea ice is a grave warning to all of us, so it's madness that companies like Cairn see it as a chance to drill for the fossil fuels that got us into this climate change mess in the first place. We have to say, 'No more.'" The protesters were later released without charge.

This is an example of direct action that confronts businesses that may be causing environmental damage. Greenpeace's aims were to disrupt the drilling and create a dramatic news story that would be seen and read all over the world. This gains publicity and helps put pressure on governments that allow oil exploration in vulnerable areas such as the Arctic.

Practical help

How can poor people in developing countries get access to cheap and sustainable energy sources? In March 2009, the Global Village Energy Partnership (GVEP International) launched a unique competition in South America and the Caribbean. Local and international businesses were challenged to think up ideas for increasing the supply of renewable, low-cost energy in the region. Here are some of the winning ideas:

- turning waste from locally produced foods such as cheese, coffee, and bananas into ethanol, which can be burned to generate heat and power
- producing gas and liquid fuel by processing old vehicle tires

- making low-cost solar water heaters from recycled materials
- developing special **turbines** to generate electricity from slow-moving rivers
- enabling shrimp fishermen to use night-lights powered by the Sun, instead of gas or oil
- inventing a system that finds the best sites for generating power from tidal currents.

Winners received grants of almost $20,000 over two years to develop their plans.

This is an example of giving practical help to the people who need it most. The ideas make little use of harmful fossil fuels and do not need huge plants or power stations to produce the power.

Protest and the law

Every country has its own laws about demonstrations and other disruptive actions. Anyone who stages protests may be acting illegally, depending on where they are. Even though their actions are nonviolent and cause no damage, protestors may end up in jail. They must be prepared to accept the consequences for what they do.

Activists from Greenpeace have landed on many oil platforms to make their protests against the effects of fossil fuels. These protestors have painted "Oil Kills" on a leg of the platform.

Making a difference

Global charities do a huge amount of work to protect our planet and its people who are under threat from pollution, climate change, and other dangers. Without them, the world's environment would be in an even worse mess than it already is. But environmental organizations can also make a huge difference in the lives of the people who work for them.

Homeless and hopeless

When he was 15 years old, Joshua Carrera and his family were evicted from their apartment. They had to live in a shelter in Brooklyn, in New York City, for nearly a year. Life was hard, and Joshua was unsure about how he would get away from the shelter, at least for the summer. "I was angry," he says. "I was confused and lost. Of all my friends, I never thought I would be the one homeless." Then he heard about a program run by the Nature Conservancy charity. Called Leaders in Environmental Action for the Future (LEAF), it offered paid internships on conservation projects for students from poor and urban areas.

Joshua applied for a place in the program but was rejected. He was devastated. The next year he applied again, and this time he was accepted as an intern. That summer he headed for the Lake Champlain valley in Vermont. It was an experience that would change his life.

An internship with the Nature Conservancy helped Joshua Carrera to change his life. He now does fieldwork and other research in threatened areas of North and South America.

Out in the wilds

Like most LEAF students, Joshua knew nothing about life outdoors in the countryside. He had rarely ever been out of the city. "Everything I knew about nature was from documentaries and the Discovery Channel," he recalled. Now, suddenly, he had to get used to long, hard days of work in the open air.

His job was finding and clearing weeds that were choking the nature reserves run by the Conservancy in Vermont. Joshua had never worked so hard in his life. "Coming from New York City, I always had the freshest pair of kicks on, I always cared about the way I dressed," he says. "Working in nature meant dressing differently and not caring about getting your hands dirty."

He also found that he enjoyed the peace and the challenges of the job, from canoeing on lakes to hiking long distances with a heavy backpack. He learned self-reliance—budgeting his money and washing his clothes. Most important of all, he found a sense of purpose he had never had before.

A career in conservation

Joshua's experiences that summer convinced him that he wanted to work with nature. He landed other internships with the Conservancy in North America. He started other charity projects of his own, such as raising money to build homes for indigenous peoples in Guatemala. He has done fieldwork research in Ecuador (where his family is from).

The Nature Conservancy

Founded in 1951, the Nature Conservancy is one of the oldest and biggest environmental charities. Its aim is to preserve the diversity of life on Earth by protecting plants, animals, and ecosystems. Based in the United States, the conservancy has projects in more than 30 countries around the world. These include grasslands in Kenya, freshwater habitats in China, and coral reefs in the western Pacific.

COMMUNITY CONSERVATION

There are several hundred big global charities devoted to the environment. However, the number of local, small-scale environmental organizations runs into several thousands. In fact, no one knows exactly how many there are all over the world. These groups usually focus on issues that directly affect their community, such as cleaner public transportation, or pollution from power stations, or threatened habitats in the area.

Small can be beautiful

Of course, local charities do not have the influence, the wide news coverage, or the money that big organizations enjoy. They have small staffs, and many of these people work for little or no pay. They can rarely afford massive publicity campaigns.

However, the smaller groups do have many advantages. By choosing a single issue, they can concentrate their attention on it completely and are often able to exert a lot of pressure on governments or corporations. By tackling environmental problems that affect the immediate community, they can appeal directly to local people. These local people may not usually get involved with charity work, but they are more likely to support campaigns on their doorstep.

Fighting for the local environment

How can communities get inspired to act on local environmental issues? Often it requires a lot of hard work from environmental groups in the area to inspire and inform people. This means not just highlighting the problems posed by pollution, global warming, habitat destruction, or other threats. The groups also have to offer practical solutions and show how they can be made to work.

Some areas of the world have especially active community groups. In the state of California, for example, dozens of local environmental organizations are campaigning for their own towns or departments to lessen their harmful impact on the environment.

Among these is the Community Environment Council (CEC) in Santa Barbara. Its major project, called "Fossil Free by '33," aims to encourage local people to stop the use of all fossil fuels in the region within a generation (by 2033). They believe this can be achieved through:

- the use of electric cars
- solar, wind, and wave energy
- building new, more efficient housing
- only buying products with a low **carbon footprint**
- and centering communities around people, not cars.

Green energy: Megan Birney

Megan Birney is part of the team running the Santa Barbara CEC. She specializes in renewable energy. She provides information to local people and business owners who want to invest in renewable sources (such as solar power) and helps the CEC support local energy projects. She gives advice to local governments about how to tackle climate change and **greenhouse gas** emissions. Megan also finds time to teach a course on renewable energy at a local college.

The Community Environment Council in Santa Barbara, California, gives advice on renewable energy to local people.

Action in focus

Smaller charities can concentrate their full attention on a single area or problem. Despite their size, their enormous range of activities can have a powerful effect on a wide variety of environmental threats. Here are some examples of how local or special-interest organizations are tackling two of today's major green issues.

Preserving the landscape

Irish Peatland Conservation Council (IPCC): The bogs (wetland areas) of northern Europe are a unique ecosystem. They not only provide a habitat for flowers and animals, but they also act as a natural storehouse for carbon and a record of past cultures and climates. For centuries, the Irish have cut peat (compacted vegetable matter) from the bogs, which was dried and burned as fuel. The IPCC protects a sample of unspoiled peatlands across Ireland, repairing damage and educating people about their importance. The council has just seven full-time employees.

Sibuyanons Against Mining (SAM): Sibuyan is one of the most beautiful and unspoiled islands in the Philippines. Since 2006, it has been threatened with extensive mining for nickel, gold, and other valuable materials. SAM has been at the forefront of opposing the mining applications from Australian and other companies, which endangered nearly half the island. It has organized petitions and mass rallies and gained support from governments and environmental charities all over the world.

Preventing pollution

Surfers Against Sewage (SAS): SAS was formed in Cornwall, England, in 1990 by surfers who were made sick by seawater polluted with sewage. Its mission was to publicize and protest against the pumping of raw sewage and other toxic waste into the sea. Since then, SAS has pressured water companies into treating their sewage. It has also tackled the problems of beach litter and dangerous pollution from shipping.

Association for the Protection of the Environment (APE) (Egypt): The huge Egyptian capital of Cairo produces an enormous amount of garbage. Much of this is gathered for free and then sorted and recycled by the people of the Mokattam area. The APE fights for the rights of these amazingly efficient garbage collectors, who recycle up to 90 percent of what they collect. The charity runs projects to improve working conditions and to make their work safer and easier—in addition to providing schools and health care.

Members of Surfers Against Sewage staged a "toilet protest" in England. This highlighted the way raw sewage is pumped directly into the oceans.

The Big Green Bus

Every summer, the Big Green Bus travels all over the United States, from Mississippi through California and Wyoming and over to New Hampshire. On board are Dartmouth College students, whose mission is to encourage Americans to help create a sustainable future. At each stop, they give people information and useful tips about renewable energy, how to cut their carbon emissions, and other environmental matters. The bus itself has been converted into an educational exhibit. It has solar panels, rechargeable batteries, and bamboo floors—and its engine runs on recycled cooking oil.

Sandwatch: Caring for the world's beaches

Grenada has some of the most beautiful beaches in the Caribbean. In the summer of 2010, these were invaded by hundreds of students. Armed with measuring tapes, microscopes, water testing kits, and garbage bags, they spread out over the sands and set to work. They cleared up litter, measured wave heights and currents, tested water quality, and made maps of beach **erosion** and vegetation.

Altogether, students from 12 Grenadian schools took part in this project. They planned to come back at least once a month to repeat their measuring and clearing. In this way, they would be able to keep watch on how the beaches altered over time through erosion, pollution, and other forces.

Global—and local

Grenada's project is part of a much bigger campaign to monitor and protect the world's beach environments, called Sandwatch. This is not a single organization, but rather a network of small, local action groups in many islands and coastal areas, covering more than 40 countries. These stretch from the Pacific islands and South America, to across Europe and Africa, all the way to eastern Asia.

Sandwatch is a true grassroots movement. It was launched in 1999 by the United Nations Educational, Scientific, and Cultural Organization (UNESCO) as a volunteer network of students, teachers, members of youth groups, and other community bodies. Its aim is to make young people aware of the fragile nature of the coastal environment and of the need to use it wisely.

How are beaches monitored?

The following are the main measurements and other activities that Sandwatch volunteers need to complete on a field trip:

- sketch a map of the beach
- measure beach erosion/**accretion** (high-water mark, taken at three places from fixed points with photos)
- study beach composition (get samples of sand for microscope/magnifying glass; note materials, color, size, and texture of grains)
- study human activity (make notes and photos of types and numbers)

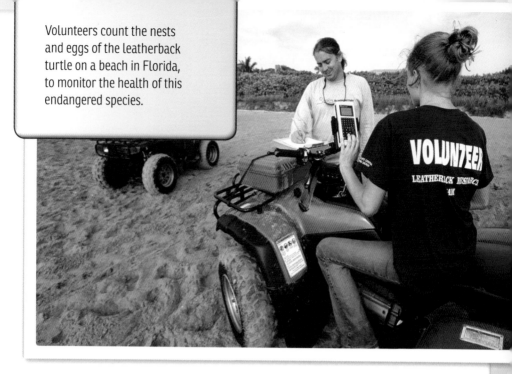

Volunteers count the nests and eggs of the leatherback turtle on a beach in Florida, to monitor the health of this endangered species.

- examine beach debris (clean the beach and note types, with photos)
- study wave characteristics (height, frequency, direction, water, and air temperatures)
- measure current (use dye markers to measure how much dye moves over 60 seconds from a fixed point in the water)
- study flora/fauna (note types of animals and plants on and around beach)
- test water (look for nitrate, phosphates, salt, and other levels).

The Sandwatch project achieves a lot in helping to conserve the world's beaches and coastal seas. But it also has other valuable benefits for local communities.

- It educates young people about the threats to the coastal environment and the importance of sustainable development.
- It reinforces schoolwork in other related areas of the curriculum, such as science and math.
- It encourages students and other community members to learn to work together.
- It empowers ordinary people to have a real and positive impact on the world around them.

Getting together

Environmental groups have many different aims and programs. But they are heading in the same general direction. They all want to make the world a healthier and fairer place, and to protect its environments and people from the likely disasters produced by climate change.

The smaller charities and nonprofit organizations sometimes find it hard to get their messages heard. However, if they work together on similar or related projects, they can make a stronger impact. This works especially well for local groups, which can take part in wide-ranging campaigns to make their communities, cities, or counties "greener."

Making it local

This can also work the other way around—with a national organization running local trusts and charities. Groundwork USA, for example, is a collection of community-based partnerships in cities all over the country. These include Dallas, Texas; Denver, Colorado; Milwaukee, Wisconsin; New Orleans, Louisiana; Portland, Oregon; and San Diego, California. Advice and organization come from its headquarters in New York City.

The trusts work to regenerate and improve their environments in many ways. They reclaim vacant land or land that is in bad shape for conservation or recreation areas. They clean up polluted brownfield (old industrial) sites and make them healthy and usable again. They encourage local businesses to support nonprofit groups.

Among Groundwork's recent achievements are:

- clearing a factory site in Minneapolis, Minnesota, so it can be used as a park and wetland reserve
- cleaning garbage and undergrowth that was choking part of the Saw Mill River, a tributary of the Hudson River
- helping schools build and maintain gardens in San Diego
- introducing an energy-efficiency program to households in Denver
- helping to construct a green trail through the center of Gary, Indiana.

Volunteers plant a garden on an industrial site on the banks of the Gowanus Canal in Brooklyn, New York. The area was targeted by the U.S. government's program to clean up the nation's uncontrolled hazardous waste sites.

A day in the life...

What is it like working as a conservation volunteer at a local charity, far from home? Here is a typical day of volunteer Jenn Beard, who worked for the Azafady Conservation Campaign out in the bush in Madagascar during 2010.

Dawn: Woken by the Sun rising and one of the cooks banging a spoon on a pot of rice. Other days we might be treated to dough balls or banana bread. After breakfast we fetch water from the well and get to washing up.

7:30 a.m.: Out into the bush to measure and study specimens of trees or lemurs, search for reptiles, build beehives, help to restore drains, clear weeds, or teach at the school.

12:00: Back to camp for lunch of rice and beans, and a rest during the hottest part of the day.

2:00 p.m.: A lesson in the Malagasy language with one of the guides. We learn about simple conversations, buying goods, and how to count and tell the time.

3:00 p.m.: Back to work—either continuing from the morning or doing something else entirely.

Sunset: Return to camp to finish anything daylight is needed for and have dinner. After dinner dishes are done we talk, play games, laugh, or just look at the stars.

EDUCATING FOR CHANGE

The most obvious work of many charities is the practical help they give. Raising money for equipment or restoring habitats is very important. But education is just as important—especially for organizations that are devoted to environmental issues. Most environmental groups see educating and informing as the first step in protecting endangered parts of the world.

Why educate?

Environmental charities have three main targets for their educational work. The first is the huge number of people in the front line who are directly affected by climate change or pollution. These include farmers, forest workers, and threatened indigenous peoples who can be given special training to help them deal with the results of environmental changes— for example, water shortages or increased flooding.

The second target is the world of industry and business. Mining and manufacturing companies, for example, have been responsible for a huge amount of carbon emissions and pollution of air, soil, and water supplies. Charities and other pressure groups have engaged with large and small companies and helped them find ways to lessen their harmful impact on the environment.

The third target is the general public. Many of the growing threats to our environment do not seem dramatically obvious. They do not hit the headlines in the way that terrible famines, droughts, or earthquake disasters do. So it is very important to inform and alert people about the dangers facing the planet from "invisible" factors, such as global warming or the crisis in energy supplies.

Learning about the environment

Education plays a major part in the structure of many environmental charities and other nonprofit organizations. Many staff members (especially those in the field) have studied environmental subjects. The charities often prefer to employ people who have gained degrees or taken classes related to the issues they deal with.

There are two major areas of learning. Environmental Science examines how Earth and its systems work. It is based on the sciences, including physics, chemistry, and biology, as well as ecology (plant and animal relationships) and geology. Environmental Studies examines how humans interact with their environment.

Send a Cow—save lives

Amsalu Haile is a farmer in one of the most remote areas of Ethiopia, in Africa. Ten years ago, his 10 children were always hungry. But then he got help from the charity Send a Cow, which trains families in natural farming methods that are kind to the environment. It also provides them with the seeds, animals, and tools they need. With Send a Cow's aid, Amsalu started to grow more food. He can now afford to pay for his children to go to school. He also works to pass on his new knowledge to help others and has trained more than 20 neighboring farmers.

Sylvie was left an orphan after civil war in Rwanda and takes care of her brothers and sisters. She was given a goat to provide vital milk by the Send a Cow charity.

Get them when they are young

Many charities have recognized the crucial importance of educating children about environmental issues. Young people who are aware of the problems threatening our planet will be better equipped to solve them in the future. For example, WWF has been helping to educate children in the United Kingdom about the environment by running a "One Planet Schools" program. This offers resources, activities, and tools for teachers and students. It helps them to get in touch with other schools around the world, share information, and coordinate lesson projects.

In the United States, the Conservation Fund is heading a campaign to reconnect children with the natural world by getting them outdoors. Called "Outdoor Nation," it sponsors clubs all over the country where kids can enjoy camping, hiking, mountain biking, gardening, and other activities.

Education

"The most important task, if we are to save the Earth, is to educate."
Peter Scott (1909–1989), founder of WWF

A visitor to the Center for Alternative Technology learns about generating power from the Sun's rays.

Changing attitudes: Greener living

How can an environmental disaster be avoided? Most environmental groups believe that humans will have to change the way they live. Everyone will need to make big changes, such as using renewable energy sources, building more efficient homes, and learning to recycle waste. To do this, they need to be taught about new attitudes and skills.

Some charities are devoted almost entirely to educating ordinary people in this way. The Center for Alternative Technology (CAT) in Wales, in the United Kingdom, offers classes in all aspects of green living, from organic food growing and woodland management to eco-sewage (toilet waste) systems and rainwater storage. Visitors can see examples of renewable energy in action, including wind turbines, solar panels, and water-powered generators.

Sustainable buildings at CAT

Emma Donnelly joined the 2011 architecture summer school run by the Center for Alternative Technology. The class teaches students about designing and constructing buildings using sustainable materials and methods. One project was to build a stand for a music festival. She says:

"It's now halfway through the summer school, and Day 1 of building a festival structure by the end of the month. There are 10 of us in the team, plus two teachers. Day 1 has been great. After our team briefing, we set about measuring, sawing, screwing, chiseling, and carrying our components. The structure is three timber-frame 'petals' 11, 14, and 18 feet [93.5, 4.2, and 5.5 meters] high. We started with the middle-sized petal. And that was pretty big! I can't wait to see the whole thing!"

The Sierra Club

The Sierra Club, founded in California in 1892, is one of the world's oldest environmental groups. Its original mission was to protect the Sierra Nevada region. Today, the club has thousands of members throughout the United States. Its educational programs aim to attract people of all generations, cultures, and abilities and to teach them how to protect the environment. The Sierra Club's education center is in Yosemite, the famous national park.

The power of the Sun: Solar Energy International

A lot of people understand that we cannot continue using fossil fuels. Many also know about the importance of harnessing the natural energy of the Sun, wind, and water to generate power instead. But very few people can actually install a solar panel or build a wind turbine, let alone make use of the electricity they produce.

Solar Energy International (SEI) was created to train people in those skills. It is a nonprofit organization that encourages people to learn the practical side of renewable energy resources. Based in Colorado, it educates and instructs people from all over the world about how to install and maintain sustainable systems of generating power. These include solar **photovoltaic cells** (PVCs) and wind and water turbines.

What does SEI do?

• *Classes and workshops in the United States*
Over the past 20 years, more than 16,000 people from all 50 states and 66 other countries have attended SEI's renewable energy classes. The organization's team of instructors has trained them to design, construct, install, connect, and maintain solar and other systems.

• *Online training*
Many of these classes can be taken online by students overseas. They have also been translated into Spanish to cater to the huge number of students from South American countries.

• *Women's classes*
To encourage more women to gain skills in renewable energy, the SEI runs special sessions that are run by women for women.

• *American Indian classes*
The SEI works with American Indian environmental groups to offer classes and provide installations for reservations. The aim is to help American Indians build new energy networks.

• *Solar in the Schools*
Children are taught the basics of renewable energy through classroom presentations by SEI instructors, while their teachers can attend workshop classes.

- *Business services*

The SEI creates classes specially suited to individual companies. It also gives help to other nonprofit organizations.

- *International programs*

Over 2 billion people in developing countries of the world have no access to modern forms of energy. The SEI has offered training classes and workshops for groups in nations across the globe, from Mexico and Ecuador, through South Africa and Palestine, to Pakistan and the Solomon Islands.

Solar panels can be fitted anywhere that gets a lots of sunlight, such as this traditional house in the Sahara Desert region of Algeria.

Hugh Piggott, wind turbine wizard

Hugh Piggott is SEI's expert on wind generators, and he works as a training instructor in workshop classes. He has been working with wind power for over 30 years and has built many turbines—the biggest was nearly 15 feet (5 meter) in diameter. Hugh has also designed small wind turbines for use in Zimbabwe, Sri Lanka, and Peru.

"I dream about wind machines all the time. We live in a world rich in free, natural energy, which is out there for the taking. There are few thrills to beat a well-engineered wind turbine working in a good breeze."

Hugh Piggott

MONEY AND PUBLICITY

Without money, charities and other nonprofit organizations would not exist. They need a constant supply of funds to pay for their projects, their offices and staff, and their fund-raising operations. At the same time, charities need publicity. It is very important that as many people as possible know about their aims and campaigns. This will bring them support—and donations.

Sources of money

Have you ever put money in an environmental charity worker's collection can? Or donated online during a national television campaign? These are obvious ways to raise cash to save the planet. But donations are just one of several sources that keep charities afloat:

• *Donations from individuals*: These are made by ordinary people passing collectors in the street, through major appeals in the media, or through sums of money left in someone's will (after they die).

• *Donations from businesses*: Many companies and corporations give regular sums to charities. Some even match the donations made by their employees.

• *Donations from charitable trusts*: People who want to set aside some of their wealth for charitable causes can set up a trust. These trusts will give money to selected charities.

• *Government grants*: National governments and international organizations (such as the UN) pay regular sums to certain charities.

• *Tax relief*: Most people and businesses have to pay taxes on the money they earn. However, many governments give charities freedom from these taxes.

• *Earned income*: A charity can earn income in many ways—through selling goods they have produced (such as books) or by selling services (such as technical training or advice).

How do charities spend their money?

Environmental charities raise their cash from public and private sources. By law, they have to account very strictly for how they spend it. Here are the figures for some big organizations mentioned in this book. It shows the percentages of their incomes they spent on their projects (practical work in the field), on administration (running the office and paying staff members), and on fund-raising and promotion (publicity and campaigns).

Where charities spend their money (in percentages)

Charity	Projects	Administration	Fund-raising	Other
Conservation Fund	97.2	1.7	0.9	0.2
Earthwatch Institute	83.4	10.3	6.1	0.2
Friends of the Earth	85.5	7.5	6.8	0.2
Nature Conservancy	77.9	13.0	9.1	N/A
Rainforest Alliance	94.1	0.8	4.9	0.2
World Land Trust	96.5	2.6	0.8	0.1
WWF	77.2	0.1	14.6	0.1

If you look closely at the table, you can see that some charities spend much more on administration or fund-raising than others. Why do you think this is? Remember that groups such as the WWF conduct a lot of publicity and press campaigns that put pressure on governments and corporations. They also encourage individuals to act—not just to donate money, but to spread news, sign petitions, and demand changes. Most of the others do not do this, so their spending patterns are different.

A charity worker recruits volunteers on the streets by providing information.

Al Gore and the Alliance for Climate Protection

One of the biggest charity success stories in recent years has been the growth of a new organization, the Alliance for Climate Protection (ACP). Surprisingly, it grew out of a failure. In 2000, Al Gore lost the race to become the U.S. president. After this, he devoted much of his time to publicizing the problems of climate change.

Most famously, Gore starred in the 2006 documentary film called *An Inconvenient Truth*. This used factual evidence to argue that climate change was caused by human activity and would lead to catastrophe if we did not change our way of life. The film became one of the most successful documentaries of all time. That same year, Gore founded the Alliance for Climate Protection.

What does the ACP do?

The ACP is not a practical charity aimed at directly helping people affected by environmental issues. It is all about publicity and **lobbying**. Its mission is to discover and call attention to the shocking reality of the climate crisis. By using modern communications (through Facebook, Twitter, and other social networking sites), it has been able to carry its message swiftly across the world.

These are the alliance's major projects:

The Climate Project
The ACP has a worldwide force of lecturers who educate people about the looming crisis of climate change and the ways to fight it. Their main campaign tool is a slide-show version of the facts from *An Inconvenient Truth*.

Repower America
This campaign calls for the United States to switch to a cleaner energy system, with more efficient energy use, power generated from renewable sources, and investment in electric cars.

The We Campaign
Launched in 2008, this urged Americans to pressure their government into making major reductions in carbon emissions.

The Climate Reality Coalition

In September 2011, the ACP teamed up with the Sierra Club and other environmental groups for a worldwide live, streamed event. Its aim was to expose the full scale of the climate crisis.

Are celebrities good for charities?

There are many nonprofit groups that campaign about climate change. So why has the ACP had such a rapid growth and gained so much publicity? This is partly due to the work of its staff and supporters. But the biggest reason is the fact that Al Gore is famous, powerful, and wealthy. He was even awarded the 2007 Nobel Peace prize for his environmental work.

Is this a good thing for the environmental movement as a whole? The ACP is certainly using enormous amounts of money in its projects. In 2008, it announced it would spend $300 million on its global We Campaign. The sum was raised thanks to Gore's contacts and the success of his books and film. Is this money that could have been given to other charities? Would the cash have been better spent on more practical projects? What do you think?

Al Gore's film *An Inconvenient Truth* has had a huge impact on world attitudes toward climate change and global warming.

Getting noticed

For their work to have an impact, environmental charities need publicity almost as much as money. They have to get their message across clearly to as many people as possible. The message might be asking for donations or new members, or drawing attention to threats to our environment. Persuasive and powerful publicity is the best way to encourage support and help the organization achieve its aims.

So, media campaigns are an important part of charity work. Most large nonprofit groups have an expert team devoted to this, with large budgets to pay for national advertising and other mass publicity. Smaller charities have less money to spend, so they have to focus their media messages on specific groups or areas.

Using the media

There is an enormous variety of news and advertising media, from newspapers and magazines to radio, TV, and social networking web sites. Publicity and press experts for charities have to carefully choose the most effective ways of employing them. How much will it cost? How many readers or viewers will it reach? Is its audience likely to be interested in the message?

Basically, publicity comes in two forms:

• *Free*: Newspapers and broadcast media are always looking for a good newsworthy story that is fresh, interesting, and unusual. Many green issues provide such stories, whether it is Greenpeace activists protesting on an oil-drilling platform or Send a Cow training farmers in Ethiopia. The charity's press expert sends out details of the story in a **press release**. If journalists are interested, they will follow it up, either in a feature article or a recorded interview. Publicity of this kind is free.

• *Paid for*: Charities can also buy publicity. They can pay for posters or magazine or TV advertisements. They can mail brochures, advertising material, and donation forms to millions of households. They can send e-mails and messages through cell phone texts and social networking sites. And they can keep their own members informed about events through newsletters and their own web sites.

Sofiyah McCormack poses with a potential new member of the Wilderness Society.

Sofiyah McCormack, Wilderness Defender Campaigner

The Wilderness Society in Australia works to protect and preserve the country's wild places, plants, and animals.

Sofiyah is a wilderness defender. Her job is to go out and meet members of the public, tell them about the organization, and encourage them to become members. Sofiyah says the most rewarding part of her work is "helping people remember how powerful we all are, and that each of us is more than capable of creating a better world."

Working for the Wilderness Society has taught Sofiyah a lot. Besides fund-raising techniques, she says she has learned "resilience, patience, and compassion. I've also met some pretty amazing people that I might otherwise have never crossed paths with." Sofiyah has had the opportunity to travel all over Australia as part of her job.

Recruiting new members brings in most of the organization's money, so the work of fund-raisers like Sofiyah is essential in helping to run publicity campaigns and carry out conservation work. Sofiyah knows how important her job is. She is helping to protect beautiful places and is proud to make a difference as part of an **ethical** organization.

RESEARCH

Advances in technology and science have had a huge impact on our lives. They have also helped cause a lot of damage to our planet over the past 200 years. For example, new machines, chemicals, and factory processes have brought pollution and global warming. But technology may also hold the solutions to these problems by developing cleaner and more sustainable ways of living.

What is research for?

To cope with or prevent environmental disaster, we have to learn more about Earth and how we affect it. Researchers provide crucial information to help with this crisis. Their work covers most environmental issues, such as:

• *Habitat conservation*: Scientists and charity field workers are studying nature reserves and other ecosystems to find practical solutions to threats such as global warming and expanding human populations.

• *Renewable energy*: Researchers, often backed by existing fossil fuel companies as well as green organizations, are developing alternative power sources that are sustainable and low in carbon emissions.

• *Pollution*: Many groups, usually those backed by national governments, have paid for projects to find practical methods to prevent toxic substances from entering soil, air, and water systems.

• *Carbon emissions*: Scientists are looking for ways to "capture" carbon emitted from power stations and other sources and store it, so it does not enter the atmosphere.

• *Food production*: A number of environmental charities support research into more sustainable farming methods, including the use of organic fertilizers, feeds, and **pesticides**.

Who pays for research?

A lot of scientific research is highly specialized work, which takes place in laboratories equipped with the latest tools and expert knowledge. Few charities have the money or space to run establishments like this. So the research is done by colleges that have the equipment and the top academic scientists.

Projects at environmental research laboratories are given financial support by charities and by **government agencies**. For example, the Environmental Change Institute at Oxford University, in England, is one of the leading green research centers in the world. Its recent projects include helping to plan the United Kingdom's long-term policies on energy and transportation. This was partly paid for by UK government groups.

The moral question

Charities have difficult choices. Many rely on large and regular donations of money from businesses of all kinds. But are these companies genuinely interested in helping the environment, or are they just anxious to be seen as "green"? Should charities accept donations from anyone? Or should they reject those companies that do not follow fair and ethical principles? For example, some nonprofit groups conduct research into new cleaner and greener fuels. Gasoline companies may help to pay for this research. Such companies have caused widespread environmental damage, through disasters such as oil spills. But their support might make the world less reliant on oil. What choice should the charity make?

Research into plant growth plays an important part in encouraging food production in threatened areas of the world.

The work of Earthwatch

The Earthwatch Institute is an environmental organization that funds projects all over the world. Its central aim is to use research to help protect Earth and its ecosystems. It believes that future decisions about the environment will have to be based on scientific study.

Bringing experts and students together

People are at the core of Earthwatch's research projects. This means not just qualified scientists and experts, but also volunteers and students with little or no experience. The institute wants to get ordinary people working in field research and education. This will help them understand the environment and what action is needed to make it sustainable.

Since the charity was founded in 1971, it has sent more than 85,000 volunteers out into the field to work alongside scientists all over the world. The volunteers pay for their adventure, and so in this way they contribute funds to the projects. But in return, they learn about conservation and the need to take responsibility for the environment. Many go home inspired to work for change in their own communities.

Where are the projects?

Here is a selection from over 100 Earthwatch research projects worldwide:

- *California*: Earthwatch has traced plant changes in response to climate change and development.
- *Mongolia*: People have discovered and documented the indigenous culture of the **steppes**.
- *Bahamas*: Earthwatch is monitoring the health of coral reefs and the impact of climate change.
- *Borneo*: Earthwatch is helping scientists assess the effect of global warming and collect data to help with restoring damaged rain forest areas.
- *Canada*: People are helping to record data from the edge of the Arctic ice, to show the effect of rising global temperatures.
- *Kenya*: Earthwatch is working with indigenous peoples to build sustainable economies and study interactions between humans and wildlife.

Volunteer on the ice

"My interest in the environment was really awakened during my time working with the charity Earthwatch. In 2006, I was a team member on their Icelandic Glaciers expedition, one of the many expeditions run by Earthwatch that allow volunteers to get directly involved in 'hands-on' environmental research," says Clare Marl.

The Skaftafell region contains the largest glacier in Europe and two huge volcanoes hidden under the ice. One of these had erupted in 1996, causing disastrous floods. Since then, a team of researchers has been closely studying the area and the impact of the natural disaster. The team had to work under extreme conditions. The weather could change suddenly from sunshine to storms, and the wind chill could lower temperatures within a few minutes.

Some of the volunteers worked on mapping and surveying changes. Some used radar to measure the depth of sand and ice. Others used satellite-positioning systems to record the speed and direction of the glacier's movement. These studies meant the researchers would be able to predict what might happen if another eruption occurred.

The volunteers learned just how sensitive glaciers are to rises in temperature, whether from volcanic eruptions or from changing climates. This makes them important indicators of global warming.

Earthwatch researchers hiked for several miles across sandy wasteland before reaching the Icelandic glacier.

Researchers at work

Research teams have many ways of operating. Some work in laboratories, some in experimental workshops, and some in live consumer surveys on the street or over the phone. Here are two contrasting research projects in two very different settings.

In the office...

"EWG Meateater's Guide Spotlights Beef's Outsize Carbon Footprint"

This headline to a press release in July 2011 by the Environmental Working Group (EWG) announced the publication of the *Meateater's Guide to Climate Change and Health*. It showed just how much our food choices can affect our environment and our health.

The evidence for the guide was gathered by EWG researchers in the organization's offices in Washington, D.C. The team was led by Kari Hamerschlag, who also wrote the final report. Kari is a senior analyst with EWC in the areas of agriculture and climate change.

The object of the research was to closely study 20 types of food through every step of production. How much carbon was emitted during the entire food cycle? Using specially designed computer programs, the team was able to calculate these "carbon footprints"—from sowing the seed, through harvesting and processing the crop, to eating the food and disposing of the waste.

The results showed that eating less meat and cheese is not only healthier, but it also causes lower greenhouse gas emissions. "By eating and wasting less meat, consumers can help limit the environmental damage caused by the huge amounts of fertilizer, fuel, water, and pesticides, not to mention the toxic manure and wastewater, that goes along with producing meat," says Kari.

...and in the wild

Peter and Emma Ashton are a husband-and-wife team who share the job of managing a nature reserve at Boolcoomatta, in South Australia. This massive reserve was bought by the conservation charity Bush Heritage in 2006. Bush Heritage manages land of special environmental value and protects its plants, animals, and habitats. "We often refer to ourselves as nature farmers," says Emma, "because we live in much the same way as any farmer, but without the stock or crops."

Boolcoomatta is a strange place to call home. It is surrounded by vast, treeless plains covered in gray saltbush and prickly acacia shrubs. And it is remote. The nearest town, Broken Hill, is over 70 miles (100 kilometers) away. There is no school nearby, so the children listen to classes over the radio.

Caring for the reserve is hard work. Peter and Emma fix fences, control predators, root out invasive plants, and generally protect the extraordinary ecosystem. They are helped by Bush Heritage's teams of ecologists and volunteers, who also carry out regular surveys of the animals and plants there. Rare species found at Boolcoomatta include the dusky hopping-mouse and the purplewood wattle tree.

This research is important for two reasons. First, it shows whether Bush Heritage is using the right conservation methods. If numbers of rare animals and plants are increasing, then the methods are clearly working. Second, the research can be used to help build up a picture of habitat conservation all over Australia. This is very valuable, because the country is already suffering from the effects of climate change.

Annette Ruzicka and Emma Ignjic from Bush Heritage enjoy a morning bush walk with the local children.

A VISION FOR THE FUTURE

Environmental action is all about the future. The object of environmental charities is to protect Earth's ecosystems and inhabitants from disastrous damage, so that future generations can have safe and healthy lives. But the threat of disaster is growing and changing all the time. Charities and other organizations will have to adapt to cope with this.

Campaigning together

Local environmental action will need to involve groups covering the whole community. This will make any campaign much more powerful, so that pressure on local and national governments, and on businesses, will be stronger. It also means that all sides of an issue will be thoroughly examined. Environmental organizations in several communities are already getting together in this way.

For example, many cities have very congested road systems. Slow road traffic harms the environment in many ways, including increased air pollution and wasting of fossil fuels. Cleaner and greener transportation networks need to be developed. This can only be done efficiently if different groups work together. They include organizations that campaign for:

- car-sharing (so fewer cars are needed)
- cleaner air (controlling emissions)
- road tolls (making drivers pay for using the roads)
- congestion charging (drivers with more polluting vehicles pay more)
- cycle paths (making the use of bicycles more attractive)
- greener public transportation (using, for example, electric tram systems).

Getting more support from industry

Many environmental charities see big business as the main enemy of the environment. Mining, oil-drilling, and manufacturing companies and industrialized farming methods have certainly caused a great deal of damage. However, large corporations have a huge amount of influence and money and cannot be ignored. They have to become a major part of the answer, instead of the problem.

Car-free paths, such as this newly opened stretch in New York, encourage people to walk or cycle to work.

The BlueGreen Alliance is one organization that is trying to bring industry and environmental groups closer together. It believes that conservation issues, such as renewable energy and other practical solutions to global warming, will transform the world economy. The alliance is building a partnership between environmental organizations and labor unions, aimed at increasing the number of jobs in the new green industries.

Using new technology

Charities depend on printed and broadcast media to get their message across to the public. But new ways of communicating are being developed all the time. Many organizations already employ methods such as online advertising and cell phone texting.

Confronting climate change globally

"No nation can address this challenge on its own. No region can insulate itself from these climate changes. That is why we need to confront climate change within a global framework, one that guarantees the highest level of international cooperation."

Ban Ki-Moon, secretary general of the United Nations

Care and affection: The international Tunza project for children

Children are the future of the environment. An American Indian proverb says: "We do not inherit the Earth from our ancestors, we borrow it from our children." So it is essential that environmental organizations send a strong message to young people about the importance of taking care of the planet in the years to come. One very successful movement is the Tunza project, run by the United Nations Environment Program (UNEP).

Making young people aware

UNEP launched the new project in 2003. *Tunza* means "to treat with care and affection" in Swahili (an East African language). The concept of the Tunza project was built around "care and affection" for Earth, and for the people on it.

The aim of Tunza is to get young people engaged with activities that help the environment and, especially, in the work done by UNEP itself. This includes becoming aware of environmental threats, learning about ways to deal with these threats, and exchanging views with other young people all over the world. With this background, the next generation of adults should be equipped to take positive action to protect their planet.

The 2011 Tunza Children and Youth Conference in Bandung, Indonesia, brought together young representatives from all over the world.

Getting together

Tunza is all about taking responsibility for the future. This means joining one of the youth networks run by the organization in many parts of the world and being active in environmental campaigns, especially those promoted by UNEP. During 2011, for example, Tunza members took part in many events involved with the International Year of the Forests, World Water Day, and the Big Help Environment Campaign.

Here are some of the other activities for Tunza members:

- *The Tunza International Children and Youth Conference on the Environment*

In September 2011, over 1,400 young people came together in Bandung, Indonesia. They met to discuss a range of environmental topics, such as a new United Nations initiative called "Reshaping Our Future Through a Green Economy and Sustainable Lifestyle." They also discussed more environmentally friendly ways of living.

- *TUNZA Magazine*

This monthly magazine is written "for youth, by youth, about youth." It contains articles about a huge variety of environmental issues, from rain forests to recycling, as well as blogs and news.

- *The International Children's Painting Competition on the Environment*

This competition is held every year and is open to children between the ages of 6 and 14. Winners are picked for each region of the world, and there are also five global winners.

What is UNEP?

The United Nations Environment Program runs conservation activities all over the world for the United Nations. It helps developing countries to adopt green policies, promotes environmental research, and organizes major conferences. UNEP's headquarters are in Nairobi, Kenya.

VOLUNTEERING

Throughout this book, we have met several people who have volunteered to work for environmental charities. We have heard about their adventures and learned about some of the work they have done. Would you like to be a volunteer? This chapter tells you about the realities of the job, the hundreds of opportunities on offer, and how to find out more.

Why be a volunteer?

In simple terms, a volunteer is someone who does unpaid work for a charity. Why do people want to do this? Research has shown that there are three main reasons:

1. *To help a cause they believe in:* Someone who feels very strongly about environmental issues, such as climate change or pollution, will be eager to take practical action. This supports the cause and connects volunteers to it. It also gives people a sense of self-worth and fulfilment.

2. *To meet other people who think the same as them*: Volunteer work brings together people who often have the same ideals. They then share the experience of working together in sometimes testing circumstances. This can create long-lasting friendships.

3. *To learn something new and valuable*: Many environmental charities offer research work, world travel, and other experiences that give people fresh knowledge about the world. Some groups even give specific training in some tasks.

What is volunteer work really like?

Charity jobs come in all shapes and sizes. Volunteers may be employed close to home—as administrators in the office, as fund-raisers on the street or on the telephone, or as helpers at charity events or rallies. This kind of work is often hard and not very glamorous. It can include simple tasks such as filling envelopes, stacking chairs, or delivering newsletters.

A lot of environmental volunteers may want jobs in the field, either at home or abroad. These involve work that may be seen as much more exciting. It could be helping scientists with their research in remote locations, such as the Amazon rain forest or the Arctic ice fields, planting trees in Indonesia, or collecting medicinal plants in Kenya.

But fieldwork is not always as exotic as that, and the job may be difficult at times. You may be working in an office or in a city, rather than the great outdoors. Or you may have to cope with bad weather and unfamiliar working conditions. Then there is the chance of homesickness if you are living in a place that is remote and strange to you. Volunteers have to be resourceful enough to cope with the bad times as well as the good.

Some quotes about volunteering

"Those who can, do. Those who can do more, volunteer."
                                                    Author unknown

"Volunteers are vital to enabling this country to live up to the true promise of its heritage."
                        Bill Clinton, U.S. president, 1993–2001

"You shouldn't go through life with a catcher's mitt on both hands. You need to be able to throw something back."
                        Maya Angelou, U.S. writer and poet

Volunteering for an environmental charity can involve many different activities, from scientific research to clearing litter.

What do you need to be a volunteer?

Whether you are doing volunteer work near home or in a foreign country, you need certain qualities and experiences to see you through. By being able to cope with widely differing situations, you will be a happier and more effective volunteer.

Charities will also be more likely to give you a job if you can prove that you have the right attitude and abilities. You should:

- be able to work hard and steadily under pressure
- be able to communicate and get along with a wide variety of people
- have some experience with working in community projects or with disadvantaged people
- be good at staying focused.

You may begin by feeling that you can change the world with your efforts, then get disappointed when things do not go exactly according to plan. Do not have unrealistic expectations, and keep concentrating on the job in front of you.

If you aim to work overseas, you should also:

- have experience working in another language. This does not necessarily mean being fluent—just able to make yourself understood. The most widely useful languages (other than English) are French and Spanish.
- have enough skill and experience to give training to others. Again, you do not have to be a qualified expert, but it helps if you have some knowledge of, for example, first aid, simple mechanics, teaching, or computer technology.
- be able to cope with being far away from home for weeks or even months.
- be happy to live in simple conditions, such as tents or huts, without running water and with unfamiliar food and manners.

How much does it cost?

Voluntary work is, of course, unpaid. There are still costs involved for things such as travel, accommodation, and food.

Green volunteers can get to many dramatic places, such as the Pyrenees mountains in France.

Some charities will cover your expenses for you, as they may be included in grants they receive from government and other sources. But others (especially smaller organizations) may expect you to pay for yourself.

If you are volunteering for an environmental charity near your home, these expenses will be very little. But if you are going overseas, charities will almost certainly ask for sums to cover food, travel, and sleeping arrangements. These costs can be as much as $100 a week or more. If you have a degree in a skill—for example, in medicine or engineering—you probably will not have to pay.

It makes sense do as much research as possible before you apply for a position. On pages 62–63 you will find a list of web sites that will give you guidance and ideas about volunteering at home and overseas.

⟩⟩ FACTS AND FIGURES

Climate change: Some facts

• Eleven of the last 12 years have been the hottest since 1850, when records began.

• Global temperatures have risen by 1.37 degrees Fahrenheit (0.76 degrees Celsius) in the past 150 years.

• The amount of carbon dioxide in Earth's atmosphere has risen by 35 percent since 1750—the start of the industrial age.

• Sea levels have been rising by an average of 0.118 inches (3 millimeters) a year since 1993. This is due not just to melting ice caps, but also to the fact that the oceans are getting warmer and expanding.

• The area covered by sea ice in the Arctic has fallen by an average of 8 percent since 1978, an area of 400,000 square miles (1,036,000 square kilometers).

• The proportion of carbon dioxide in Earth's atmosphere has increased from 280 parts per million before the industrial age (*c.* 1700 BCE) to 382 parts per million in 2006. Most of the increase is due to human activity.

• During the period from 1900 to 2006, there was an increase in rainfall over North America, Europe, and northern Asia. But rainfall decreased over land between the tropics. At the same time, the Sahel region and southern Africa, as well as parts of southern Asia, became drier.

• There were 27 full-scale storms recorded during the Atlantic hurricane season of 2005. This is more than ever before.

• Since about 1700, the oceans have become more acidic. Scientists believe this is the result of increased carbon dioxide emissions due to human activity. This acidity restricts the growth of corals, shellfish, and other sea creatures.

Volunteer statistics

United States: 63.4 million adults (26 percent of the population) volunteered to help their community, giving 8.1 billion hours of service (2009 figures).

United Kingdom: 29.1 million adults (41 percent of the population) volunteered to help their community; 42 percent of these were women and 38 percent were men (2009 figures).

Australia: 5.2 million adults (34 percent of the population) took part in volunteer work, giving 713 million hours to the community; 36 percent of these were women and 32 percent were men (2006 figures).

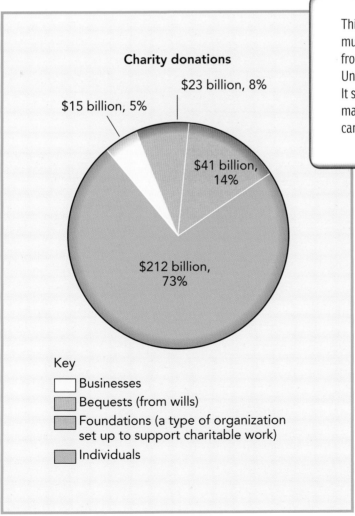

Charity donations

$23 billion, 8%

$15 billion, 5%

$41 billion, 14%

$212 billion, 73%

Key
- Businesses
- Bequests (from wills)
- Foundations (a type of organization set up to support charitable work)
- Individuals

This is a pie chart of how much was donated, and from what source, in the United States in 2010. It shows that the vast majority of donations came from individuals.

GLOSSARY

accretion buildup of material such as sand or shingle

activist someone who uses strong and direct action to campaign for a cause

agrofuel fuel made from crops that are specially grown for the purpose (also known as biofuel)

archive place where public records or historical documents are kept

biodiversity wide variety of biological forms in an area, such as plants, animals, birds, and insects

budget summary of income and expenses over a given period

carbon one of the most common elements, which occurs in many forms. It can combine with oxygen (another element) to form carbon dioxide. Carbon is one of the main causes of global warming.

carbon footprint calculation of the amount of carbon used or emitted on behalf of a person or organization

degradation ruining of farmland by pollution, or the loss of soil fertility by other causes

developed country one of the richer countries of the world, including Australia and countries in North America and Europe

developing country one of the poorer countries of the world, including the countries of Africa, Asia (except for Japan), Latin America, and the Caribbean

economy managing of money and other resources of a country or business

ecosystem community of plants and animals, together with their environment

emission giving off of exhaust gases or other materials

erosion wearing away of soil or rock by the wind, the sea, or other forces

ethical fitting in with a code of morals or behavior

food sovereignty right of people to a supply of healthy food produced by clean and sustainable methods

fossil fuel fuel, such as coal or petroleum, that was created by the decay of ancient vegetation or animals

global warming rise in the temperature of the atmosphere, caused mainly by climate change

government agency organization set up by a national government to perform a specific activity

greenhouse gas gas such as carbon dioxide that builds up in Earth's atmosphere, absorbing heat from the Sun and thus causing a rise in temperature. Greenhouse gases are a major cause of climate change.

habitat type of environment in which an animal, plant, or other organism lives

ice cap covering of snow and ice (as, for example, at the North and South poles)

indigenous native, or living naturally in an area

intern person employed to learn a business or skill, often without pay

lobby conduct activities aimed at influencing public officials

monitor watch and study carefully and keep records of something

nonprofit organization body that does not distribute its surplus income or funds, but uses them to finance its projects

nuclear energy energy made by splitting the nucleus (central part of an atom) of a uranium atom

pesticide chemical that is sprayed on the ground to destroy animal and insect pests that harm crops

photovoltaic cell cell that converts the rays of the Sun directly into electricity

pollution spoiling or poisoning of air, water, or soil with harmful substances

press release announcement of an event or other news given to the media (newspapers, TV, and radio)

radioactive giving out radiation in the form of electronic particles from uranium and other unstable elements, or from a nuclear reaction

solar energy system that uses the energy of the Sun to produce heat or electricity

steppe large, flat area of land with grass and very few trees, found in eastern Europe and Asia

sustainable something that will not run out and can be renewed, such as an energy source

turbine machine that is turned by flowing energy, such as wind or water, and converts this energy into electricity

wetland lowland area, such as a marsh or swamp, that is permanently wet

⟫ FIND OUT MORE

Here are some suggestions for discovering more information about environmental charities and the causes that they support. You will find much more information online or at your local library or bookstore.

Books

Bailey, Jacqui. *What's the Point of Being Green?* Hauppauge, N.Y.: Barron's Educational, 2010.

Benduhn, Tea. *Solar Power* (Energy for Today). Pleasantville, N.Y.: Weekly Reader, 2009.

Fridell, Ron. *Earth-Friendly Energy* (Saving Our Living Earth). Minneapolis: Lerner, 2009.

Morris, Neil. *Saving Energy* (Green Kids). Laguna Hills, Calif.: QED, 2008.

Rohmer, Harriet. *Heroes of the Environment: True Stories of People Who Are Helping to Protect Our Planet.* San Francisco: Chronicle, 2009.

DVDs

The Eleventh Hour, starring Leonardo di Caprio (Warner, 2008)
This movie documents the dangers facing many of the planet's life systems.

An Inconvenient Truth, featuring Al Gore (Paramount, 2008)
This film formed an important part of Gore's campaign to publicize the dangers of global warming.

The Truth About Climate Change, featuring David Attenborough (Eureka, 2008)
The famous naturalist travels the world to find shocking evidence of climate change.

Web sites

www.charitynavigator.org
This web site has more figures about charity spending.

www.childrenoftheearth.org/index.htm
This is a fun-filled environmental education site.

www.dosomething.org
www.volunteermatch.org
These web sites have information about volunteering possibilities and can help you find the best match for your interests and goals.

www.ecokids.ca

This site has games, stories, pictures, and facts about the environment.

www.energystar.gov

Find tips on simple ways to save energy at home.

www.forbes.com/2010/06/30/oprah-jolie-pitt-letterman-philanthropy-personal-finance-celebrity-charities.html

Find out more about the pros and cons of celebrities' involvement with charities.

www.goabroad.com/volunteer-abroad

This is a useful way to explore opportunities for volunteering in other parts of the world.

www.kidsforsavingearth.org

This offers a wide range of resources and links for teachers and parents.

money.howstuffworks.com/economics/volunteer/information/volunteer-vacations.htm

This is a straightforward guide to volunteering, backed by the charity YouthNet.

planetgreen.discovery.com/work-connect/

Get help and advice about choosing a charity to donate to.

www.unep.org/tunza

Find out more about Tunza projects on the UNEP web site.

Some major environmental organizations:

Friends of the Earth: **www.foei.org**

Greenpeace: **www.greenpeace.org/international**

The Nature Conservancy: **www.nature.org**

The Rainforest Alliance: **www.rainforest-alliance.org**

The Sierra Club: **www.sierraclub.org**

WWF: **www.worldwildlife.org**

INDEX

ActionAid 8, 16
activists 9, 12, 13, 20, 21
Alliance for Climate Protection (ACP) 40–41
alternative energy 12, 16, 20–21, 25, 35, 36–37, 40, 44

beach environments 26, 27, 28–29
BlueGreen Alliance 51

campaigns 12, 13, 40, 42
carbon emissions 16, 32, 40, 44, 48, 58
carbon footprints 25, 48
career opportunities 14, 32
Center for Alternative Technology (CAT) 34, 35
charity spending patterns 39, 41
climate change 4, 6, 7, 12, 13, 25, 32, 40–41, 46, 47, 48, 49, 51, 58
community conservation action 18, 24–31, 50

developing countries 20, 53

Earthwatch 39, 46–47
ecosystems 6, 13, 15, 17, 18, 19, 23, 26, 44, 46, 49, 50
educational work 8, 27, 29, 32–37, 40
energy crisis 6, 12, 32

farming 6, 12, 16, 17, 33, 44, 48
food sovereignty 12
forest resources 9, 12, 16, 18–19

fossil fuels 6, 12, 16, 21, 25, 36, 50
Friends of the Earth 8, 12–13, 39
fund-raising 10, 11, 38–39, 43, 45

global warming 6, 7, 12, 13, 16, 32, 46, 47, 58
Gore, Al 40, 41
grants 38, 57
greenhouse gases 25, 48
Greenpeace 9, 16, 20, 21

habitat conservation 8, 18–19, 26, 43, 44, 48–49
habitat loss 9, 12, 13, 18

indigenous peoples 19, 23, 46
industry, partnerships with 50–51
information and communications technology 40, 51
internships 14–15, 22–23

land degradation 6, 16
local green issues 8, 24–27, 30, 50

mining 12, 13, 26, 32, 50

Nature Conservancy 22–23, 39
nuclear energy 9, 11, 16

oil exploration 20, 21, 50

pollution 4, 5, 6, 16, 26, 27, 32, 44, 50
population growth 6
publicity 20, 38, 40, 41, 42, 43, 51

Rainforest Alliance 16, 39
rain forests 16, 18–19
recycling 26, 27, 35

Sandwatch 28–29
scientific research 44–49
sea level rise 6, 7, 58
Sierra Club 35, 41
Soil Association 16
solar energy 16, 21, 25, 27, 36, 37
sustainable future 27, 35, 44, 50–53

Tunza project 52–53

United Nations Environment Program (UNEP) 6, 52, 53

volunteers 4–5, 9, 10, 28, 29, 31, 46, 47, 49, 54–57, 59

Wilderness Society 16, 17, 43
wildlife habitats 17, 19, 48–49
World Land Trust (WLT) 18–19, 39
WWF 16, 34, 39

young people 28, 29, 34, 52–53